# FROM THE OTHER SIDE

# From the Other Side

## K. WALTER

# CONTENTS

1

2

3

shelf
4

battleground
6

pieces
7

24-8
8

lesson

10

running

11

ease

12

space

13

what love isn't

14

story

15

wild

16

fall

17

checking in

18

christmas

20

mother

22

beliefs

24

insight

26

subtle

27

you

28

her

30

reminder

31

falling

33

coffee

34

over

35

reminder 2

36

PTSD

37

rebuilding

38

roadmap

40

hidden

42

valentine

43

both

44

the collapse

45

love?

46

storms

47

my love

48

ABOUT THE AUTHOR - 49

From The Other Side

for those who inspire me
for those who have helped me

# SHELF

I put you on the highest shelf
in the corner
hoping that if kept
out of sight
long enough
I would heal
but your presence
was enough
to disrupt any progress made
I gathered all the loose ends
tucked them back into place
but you kept unraveling them
using them to
tie me down
before returning to your shelf
returning to a safety that

you'd never let me know
to watch me gather
myself again
as though the one hundredth time
cleaning up this mess
would be different than the ninety-ninth

# BATTLEGROUND

my body is a battleground
and my mind's been waging
war against itself
with flashfloods of memories
and landmines mistaking
reminders for touch

# PIECES

you could never love all of me
intent on breaking me down
into pieces that were more manageable
and for far too long
I allowed myself to
be fractured
for your comfort

## 24-8

24 hours avoiding
23 reactions from
22 instances where I was made to feel weak
21 spent running from
20 mistakes found holding
onto the idea that
love would save me
heal my
19 scars from the person who
protected everyone else but
me at
18 leaving after
17 times screaming that I would finally
be free from
16 years passed since the
15 minutes that robbed me of

safety found in
14 years avoiding unlocked doors
searching for
13 ways to escape
12 months waiting for the year that would
break me with
11 flashbacks from
10 years spent in that house and
9 ways I called out for help
to stop
what started
at
8

# LESSON

I went back to school
registered for every class
taught by you
focused on learning
how to earn your smile
studied each thought line
made notecards on your history
ready for pop quizzes that never happened
because I was never meant
to be there

# RUNNING

and so I run away from every source
of pain
and sit alone
wondering how I can
run away
from myself

# EASE

you loved the world with such ease
    took in the broken gave them pieces
        of your own heart
    to remind them of the beauty
        that comes from falling apart
you stole mirrors and taught the world
    about inaccuracies in reflections
        leading only to doubt
    pointing out values that
        were often looked past
    electric eyes, warm soul
    loved beyond the judgement cast
you loved the world with such ease
    and left me wondering why
                you couldn't
                        love me

# SPACE

it's hard to leave spaces that accept me for
*all* that I am
to enter spaces that expect me to be
*half* of myself
for *their comfort*

# WHAT LOVE ISN'T

love is not
    denying yourself
        to make others happy

# STORY

my body tells a story
if you listen with intent to understand
but you're set on looking
for the final page
left looking for my least messy days
where I'm more certain of us
more assured by touch
where love feels less like work
you'd like to skip the long chapters
tired of reading though the hurt
skip the pain
show only the laughter
those chapters are there, too
if you'll stay with me
long enough to see
I'm more than these disasters

# WILD

hide your wild mild is easier
to hold us back

we're told that calm is better
than weathering these

storms meant to tear down walls
built around

keeping
women
mild

# FALL

so this year I will change with
the leaves
though I have yet to learn
to fall
with such
   *grace*

# CHECKING IN

when you said you loved me
I
wasn't
me
I
was
made of pieces of women
who I knew you wanted me to be
I hid my scars
and kept my hair long
I stopped doing the things
that brought me joy
because they were the things that
worried you most
I checked at every stop to see
if you still loved "me"

I decided that I no longer loved
who I turned out to be
slowly, I found myself again
pieced her back together
but still I checked to see if you cared
I inked my skin and checked
cut my hair and checked
attended to my past
and I stopped checking
I finally recognized the person in the mirror
and loved her more than checking to see
if you would still care

# CHRISTMAS

each year the gift of silence grows louder
disguised as presents
and charismatic entrances as
*you*
become the victim in
my mother's eyes
as her focus shifts only
to how coldly I respond to the
ways you force kindness
and silence
as though it re-grafts
this branch onto the
family
tree
poisoned
by the word

*family*
knowing everything
it's not

# MOTHER

I watched as you defined
what it meant to be
a woman
wife
mother
centered around measuring the love given
priding yourself on who
others turned out to be
I watched as you disregarded that we could be
anything other than your
direct definitions of
woman
wife
mother
centered on counting the sacrifices made
as though love had a score to keep

I watched as you defined
what it meant to be
a woman
understood that it meant
giving up myself for others
learned too quickly what others would take
but your definitions told me that
sacrifices had to be made
I watched as you defined
what it meant to be
a woman
and knew I would never fit your definition
so I became more

# BELIEFS

I don't believe in God
but I fold my hands and pray
that you never look in the mirror
hating your own reflection
not because of societies expectations
of size or sought-after features
but because of a resemblance to
the person who carelessly
exchanged your innocence for
a lifetime of nightmares
I pray that you never know
what it is like to lose sight
of yourself
to see instead a face that is too similar to his
one that reminds you that
you

are still damaged
still affected
still carrying the weight
that was dropped on you
at eight
while being reassured that
this
was
normal
I pray that you never know
what it is like to stop caring
for yourself when that
reflection is too jarring
when washing your face
becomes a challenge to see if
maybe the next time it would be cleaner
maybe it would look different
maybe it would look less like his
and more like mine
and instead I'm left with scars
as reminders of all the times
I tried

# INSIGHT

you see violence in
             self-preservation
and love in
             silent destruction

# SUBTLE

loving him became an
act of self-hatred
so subtle
that it could be
done daily

# YOU

I never wanted to be seen
was content with
hiding
in the crowd
until I saw
you
bold
open
visible
vulnerable
authentically
you
setting my soul on fire
burning with wanting
more life
more me

more
you
with eyes that seem to
look through every wall I put in place to protect
my fragmented self
while I learned
who
I
was
you
with laughter that woke parts of me I laid to
rest years ago
left them wanting to come out
to see you
bold
open
visible
vulnerable
everything I always denied wanting
until now
until
you

# HER

I spent so many years
looking for him
trying to force things into place
thinking that
if only I could love him harder
it could work
but I kept finding that
I lost myself
loving him
because all along
I was
looking for *her*

# REMINDER

like a video stuck
in a constant loop
our first kiss plays
continuously
reminding me of all the ways
I would do it differently
if I could
more softly
sweetly
slowly
as though we could stay in
that moment for a lifetime
without agendas pulling
us back to reality
I relive the moment
in my head

hoping only
that the chance
will come
for a second

# FALLING

I find myself
looking for poetry
to send you
looking for the
right combination
of the right words
to tell you
that you were on my mind
because I lose all ability
to arrange the words myself
when I remember the way your eyes change
when you look at me

# COFFEE

morning coffee could never compare
to the warmth of your lips
on a cold October morning

# OVER

even when this ends
every memory will remain
written forever
exactly as it was then

# REMINDER 2

a reminder that there was
*always*
second guessing after every moment
as I was
*never*
enough

# PTSD

sentenced to a lifetime of landmine memories
detonating at the slightest touch
with no promise of probation
you are prisoner to a mind
trapped by every decision someone else made

# REBUILDING

you will ask me how I am and
I give you the best answer I can
that I am alive
that I am busy
that I don't know how to let you in
I don't know how to uncover the years
of telling you that I was okay
of telling you that I had nothing to tell you
because I didn't know how to point out
all the things that you did not notice
how to tell you that
while you took a break for yourself
while you took care of others
you missed me
you missed him
you missed the times I called out for help

the silence, the scars
the way eating became a way to
finally have control
the way silence became routine
now I don't know how to let you in
how to tell you anything other than
I am alive

# ROADMAP

this town turned road map of every first
look
turned
longing
turned first kiss
turned
love wasn't supposed to feel
like
this
crossroad with no clear direction
on who was supposed to
go first
*no, you go first*
where stop meant go

and go meant
*don't leave*
but don't leave
meant
*leave* but
*don't confess*
the misdirection
so it can be done
again

# HIDDEN

street light glow
parking lot nights
were the only place
you could risk
loving me

# VALENTINE

sitting in silence
you asked me to abandon myself
for you
and I
staring at the ceiling
asked if we would celebrate
Valentine's Day
as though I could love you
into treating me better

# BOTH

how confusing it is
to be both
   *too much*
and
   *not enough*

# THE COLLAPSE

in the quiet midnight
hour dim lights exposed
the crumbling family
structure as
hands stopped holding
and began grasping for
the past
they thought they knew
decade old secrets
pouring out
in landslide waves
with no plan in place
to lessen the destruction

the collapse was inevitable

# LOVE?

I watched as you
turned love into ammunition
directed at destroying
everything I had to offer

# STORMS

I thought I knew
of storms
until I met her

# MY LOVE

let me rearrange
lines of stolen
poetry
carefully
to sing your praise

K. Walter currently resides in Montana and enjoys writing, travel, work, and time with loved ones including her cat, Rucker, who likes to contribute to the writing process by stepping on keyboards. She also enjoys running off to mountain cabins with her typewriter to rework her poems. From the Other Side is her first collection of poetry that looks back upon life challenges while attempting to leave an open element for reader interpretation.